Ringneck Parakeets

A Complete Ringneck Parakeet Care Guide

Ringneck Parakeets Facts & Information, where to buy, health, diet, lifespan, types, breeding, fun facts and more!

By Lolly Brown

Foreword

The Ringneck Parakeet has a history that dates back to as early as 200 B.C. and they have been kept as exotic pets for over thousands of years. One of the most significant parakeet owners in history was Alexander the Great!

Ringneck parakeets were admired by bird enthusiasts for their colors and charming dispositions. They are very intelligent creatures and are fond of flying and exploring the world around them.

Although parakeets are a great choice as pets, these birds doesn't come with a thin instruction manual, but fear not! In this book you'll be easily guided on understanding your Ringneck parrot, their behaviors, their characteristics, how you should feed and care for them and a whole lot more.

Embark on the wonderful journey of sharing your life with a Ringneck Parakeet. Learn to maximize the great privilege of living with one and be able to share this unique and unforgettable experience just like the ancient heroes that came before you!

Table of Contents

Chapter One: Introduction

Ringneck Parakeets are one of the most likeable kinds of parrots among bird enthusiasts because of their appealing colors, intelligence and outgoing personalities, not to mention their undeniable high-pitch sweet voices!

These birds have a reputation of being very sociable and interactive to people, they can adapt well in captivity and adjusts easily to a normal human lifestyle. They're also generally low maintenance compare to other birds, which makes them a very ideal pet bird.

They are recognized in four distinct subspecies: the *African Rose-ringed, Abyssinian Rose-ringed, Boreal Rose-ringed* and the most popular of them all, the *Indian Rose-ringed Parakeet*. All of which are distributed in over 24 countries around the world! Later on in this book, you will learn where and how to acquire these oh-so-sweet birds from legitimate breeders.

Ringneck Parakeets are very ideal as your first bird or pet. Although, these birds are generally easy to care for, they still require time and lots of attention so that they won't get depressed; depression could lead to undesirable behaviors among birds, and you don't want that to happen right?

Ringneck Parakeets are also in it for the long haul; these birds have a lifespan of possibly over 35 years!

They're great longtime companions, and because of that you need some guidance on how to take care of them, raise them and possibly learn how to be like them as well as teach them to be like you!!

Fortunately, this ultimate guide will teach you on how to be the best Ringneck owner you can be! Inside this book, you will find tons of helpful information about Ringneck Parakeets: how they live, how to deal with them and realize the great benefits of owning one!

Glossary of Important Terms

Avian – Pertaining to birds.

Asymptomatic – having or showing no symptoms of disease

Beak – The mouth of a bird consisting of the upper and lower mandibles.

Breast – The chest of a bird located between the chin and the abdomen.

Breeding – an act of producing young animals

Brood – a group of young birds all born at the same time.

Chick – A newly hatched bird; a baby bird.

Clutch – The eggs laid by a female bird in a single setting.

Cuttlebone – the shell of a cuttlefish that is used for supplying cage birds with lime and salts.

Flock – A group of birds.

Hatching – The process through which baby birds emerge from the egg.

Hatchling - A newly hatched chick.

Incubation – The act or process of keeping eggs warm which causes it to eventually hatch.

Mimicry – The activity or art of copying the behavior or speech of other people.

Mutation – a change in the genes of a plant or animal that causes different physical characteristics from what is normal.

Nares – the openings of the bird's nose or nasal cavity.

Pinfeathers – a not fully developed feather emerging from the skin

Sexual Dimorphism – Referring to physical differences between the sexes of the same species.

Suppler – ability to bent or twist easily

Stargazing – a twisted back in birds.

Taxonomy – The classification of species into order, family, genera, etc.

Tetra-Chromic – four color light vision including ultraviolet.

Urates – a salt of uric acid.

UVA – a radiation that causes tanning of the skin.

UVB – a radiation that is responsible for sunburn in the skin.

Wingspan – distance from the tip of one wing of a bird to the tip of the other wing.

Chapter Two: Ringneck Parakeets in Focus

Before getting a colorful and exotic bird as your pet, it's very important that you know what it is inside out!

Like many other things, you need to have proper knowledge and invest a significant amount of time to truly study and understand where these birds are coming from. That is how you will determine if this kind of pet is the right choice, so that you know what you are dealing with. In this chapter you will learn facts about Ringnecks as well as its overall characteristic.

1.) What are Ringneck Parakeets?

Ringneck Parakeets are also known and referred to as *Rose-ringed parakeets*. These birds are native to Asia and Africa and can live up to 30 years! They are highly intelligent, energetic and fun creatures which makes them a great choice as pets. These parrots had been around since 200 B.C., and because of their mimicking ability they were highly regarded by wealthy Indian royals as sacred beings!

Ringnecks are medium in size with elegant beautiful markings that also comes in different colors like blue bright yellow and green as well as other range of colors through mutation. Ringneck parrots have four subspecies; these are *African Rose-ringed, Abyssinian Rose-ringed, Boreal Rose-ringed* and the most popular of them all, the *Indian Rose-ringed Parakeet.*

These birds love to fly and mimic human speech, although mimicking is not their strongest asset, they can quickly learn to speak, whistle and imitate other sounds. Aside from flying, they are also fond of chewing and can be taught to perform tricks! Now that's entertaining!

Most Ringneck parakeets are generally easy to train and have charming personalities as long as you provide them with adequate attention, interaction, and love. They can easily become part of the family and a loving companion if you are willing to put in the time and effort to take care of them.

2.) Facts About Ringneck Parakeets

Ringneck Parakeets are scientifically known as *Psittacula krameri manillensis,* most of them originated in Asia particularly in India. In the wild they can survive in dry climates, and in captivity, they adapt well in urban development. Parakeets have an extensive range reaching in Sri Lanka and the Indian Sub-Continent.

These parrots' population exists in at least 24 countries worldwide such as United Kingdom, Spain,

France, Germany, Pakistan, Afghanistan, Japan, Vietnam, South America and the United States particularly in California, Florida and Hawaii.

Their average size including tails are about 16 - 18 inches, their wings are 153 – 180 mm long, composed of 12 feathers, with a wingspan of 15 – 17 cm and weighs about 115 –140 grams. It has an average lifespan of 25 – 35 years, although there had been some instances that these parakeets live for as long as 50 years!

Ring-necks are sexually dimorphic; males can be identified by the three bands of color or rings around their necks, while females may be seen with a very pale ring, however, they usually do not have a colored band like males. Ring-necks generally have a slender body with smooth feathers and a shiny beak.

These parrots are not picky eaters but they are strictly herbivorous and usually feed on vegetables, seeds, flowers and fruits.

In terms of reproduction, Ringnecks only brood once a year; females' clutch size ranges from 2-6 but on average they lay 3-4 eggs and incubation lasts for about 22 – 24 days.

Ringnecks also do a variety of vocalizations and can be quite a singer! Don't forget to leave them with tunes!

Quick Facts

- **Taxonomy**: phylum *Chordata*, class *Aves*, order *Psittaciformes*, family *Psittaculidae*, Genus *Psittacula*, Species *Psittacula krameri manillensis*
- **Distribution**: India, Sri Lanka, Africa, Asia
- **Habitat**: Tropical; Terrestrial
- **Anatomical Adaptations**:
- **Eggs**: 3 to 4 eggs per season
- **Incubation Period**: 22 - 24 days
- **Average Size**: 16 - 18 inches from head to tail
- **Average Weight**: 115 –140 grams
- **Wingspan**: 15 – 17 cm
- **Feather Count**: 12
- **Coloration**: green, blue, yellow, purple (through mutations)
- **Sexual Dimorphism**: Males distinctively has three bands of color or rings around their necks; Females sometimes have a very pale ring but do not have a colored band on their necks.
  Diet: vegetables, seeds, flowers, fruits.
- **Vocalization**: mimicry; choruses
- **Lifespan**: 25 – 30 years

3.) Ring-neck Parakeets in History

Parakeets have a history that dates back to as early as 200 B.C., they have been kept as exotic pets for over thousands of years. One of the most significant parakeet owners in history was Alexander the Great; he brought a parakeet to Europe from India after his conquests around 327 B.C. that is why the Alexandrine Parakeet was named after him. Parakeets were also considered sacred beings by Indian royalties because of their mimicking ability.

Some of the earliest references and historical accounts to these birds dates back to 367 B.C., from a Greek historian, named Ctesias of Cnidus. In a work he wrote called "Indica," he mentioned a bird that looks like a Sparrow-Hawk, with a greenish-blue color, a purple face and a black beak, which could also talk in an "Indian" language, because he was in India at the time.

Another literature reference to parakeets came from one of the earliest "bird care guide" book published in 72 A.D by Pliny the Elder, a Roman Scholar wherein he wrote about how to take care and train parakeets.

When the New World was discovered around the 1400's, parakeets became quite popular; bird explorers and European naturalists began further expanding their knowledge which resulted to volumes of literature on exotic birds and parrots in the late 1800's.

In the 1900's parrots became popular in the United States. A large increase in aviculture and breeding parakeet species continued from the 1930's until 1960's.

In 1979 Herbert R. Axelrod, a renowned tropical fish expert, proposed the importation of many parrot species that were previously not available.

Today, many parakeet species including Ringneck parrots are successfully bred and readily available in local pet stores and avian breeders.

4.) Types of Ringneck Parrots

There are 4 subspecies of Ringneck Parakeets; these are African Rose-ringed, Abyssinian Rose-ringed, Boreal Rose-ringed and the Indian Rose-ringed Parakeet.

The African Rose-ringed and the Indian Rose-ringed Parakeets were two of the most common types of Ringnecks available and are very ideal as pets. The Abyssinian Rose-ringed and Boreal Rose-ringed were usually endemic in other countries such as Somalia, Ethiopia and Northern India, although its population also exists both in United States and Great Britain, these types of Ringneck prefers to live in the wild.

Take a closer look at the table and do a comparison to see which type you prefer.

Indian Ring-neck vs. African Ring-neck

Indian Ring-neck	African Ring-neck
Origin: Originated from the southern Indian subcontinent.	**Origin:** Originated from western Africa and Southern Egypt.
Colour: It is dark green in colour and has a red beak.	**Colour:** It is lime green and has a purple-colored beak.
Signature Ring:	**Signature Ring:**

Rose-colored ring are prominent.	Black-ring around males are prominent.
Size and Weight: It measures 16 inches and weighs about 110 to 120 grams.	**Size and Weight:** It measures 11 to 13 inches and weighs about 120 to 125 grams.
Behaviours: They tend to be more aggressive; they bite and scream.	**Behaviours:** They are not aggressive; likes to sit on their owners' shoulders and enjoys being petted.

Abyssinian Ring-neck vs. Boreal Ring-neck

Abyssinian Ring-neck	Boreal Ring-neck
Distribution: Northwest Somalia, Sudan, Ethiopia	**Distribution:** Pakistan, Nepal, Burma, India
Colour: Its face is pale green; with	**Colour:** It has a pale grey coloring

grey-white tinge in the body; upper beak is red with a black tip.	that appears on their breasts, with red upper mandible and black markings on lower mandible.
Signature Ring: The males have a rose-colored ring; female's ring is emerald-green in color.	**Signature Ring:** It has a shade of blue limited to a narrow band at the nape.
Size: It measures approx. 40 centimeter or 15.7 inches.	**Size:** It measures approx. 43 centimeter or 16.9 inches.
Habitat: Prefers tropical habitats that are lightly forested.	**Habitat:** Prefers tropical forest as well

5.) *Colour Mutations*

Ringnecks are known for their pleasant and appealing colors. Green is the original color of this bird species. Most colors, however, have been produced in captivity; the rarer the color or mutation, the higher the price of these birds.

Sex-Linked Colors

The following colors are mutated through the male birds because they carry two color genes:

- Lutino
- Cinnamon
- Albino

Dominant Colors

The following colors came from dominant genes. It requires only one parent to be the carrier so that it will be visible with its offspring:

- Green
- Grey

Recessive Colors

The following colors came from recessive genes. This requires both parents' mutation gene to be visible with its offspring:

- Blue
- Pied
- Violet

Chapter Three: To Buy or Not to Buy?

After learning what a Rose-ringed parakeet is, where they come from and how they live. This chapter will focus on giving you practical tips on what you need to know before buying one.

You will get a whole lot of information on its pros and cons, its average monthly costs as well as the things you need so that you will be well on your way to becoming a legitimate Ringneck Parakeet pet owner, should you decide to be one! It's up to you! Read on!

1.) *Pros and Cons of Ringneck Parakeets*

The information listed below is the advantages and disadvantages of owning a Ringneck Parakeets:

Pros

- **Personality:** They are energetic, playful and very intelligent
- **Appearance:** Very colorful and appealing to the eyes
- **Noise:** They have a high but sweet and clear voices
- **Cost:** They are not that expensive compare to other birds; low maintenance
- **Speaking Ability:** They can speak very well and a quick learner
- **Impact on Humans:** You will find yourself constantly learning about these creatures. It will be an educational experience for you!

Cons

- **Personality:** They are quite difficult to tame and likes to bite.
- **Damage to Your Home**: Untrained Ringnecks could potentially chew your electric wires which could cause fires in the house. Do not leave them out of the cage and unattended.

- **Behavior:** Ringnecks tend to get jealous with other birds or family members; prone to attacking other pets and people if they feel threatened. Socializing your bird is highly recommended to avoid jealousy and aggression.
- **Noise:** Ringnecks are natural screamers and can be quite noisy at times. They love to screech too much

2.) *Ringneck Parakeets Behavior with other pets*

There is actually no general rule when introducing your pet parrot with other types or species of birds, sometimes they'll get along, sometimes they won't. When it comes to Ringneck Parakeets, it is ideal to introduce your parrot with its own kind.

Ringnecks tend to get along well with other ringneck parrot. Of course, you can introduce other types of birds but do so with caution so that they could easily warm up with their new feathered friend.

Young ringnecks often get along with other birds because they are still vulnerable to change and can adapt easily as long as you train them to accept new members.

Ringnecks, like other birds are highly individual, experts suggest that the best behaved parakeets are those who were exposed to lots of change in the environment and the ones who was trained to socialize with people because they become more adjusted.

3.) Ease and Cost of Care

Owning Rose-ringed parrot is very inexpensive; however, the supplies needed in keeping one will definitely add up to your daily life expenses, if you want to keep parakeet as a pet you should be able to cover the necessary costs it entails.

In this section you will receive an overview of the expenses associated with purchasing and keeping a Ringneck parakeet as a pet.

a.) Initial Costs

The initial expenses associated with keeping a Ringneck as pets include the cost of the bird itself as well as the cage, cage accessories, toys, and grooming supplies. You will find an overview of these costs below as well as the estimated total expense for keeping an Ringneck Parakeet:

Purchase Price: starts at $100 - $500

The price for purchasing a Ringneck is generally low and it also depends on the size of the bird, some Ringnecks are small which is cheaper and some are medium-sized which could cost more. Ringnecks who are mutated with different colors could have more value, the rarer the color is, the more expensive it gets.

Cage: starts at $170-$350

You will need a tall, strong and secure cage. You should buy something that preferably has lots of space suitable for cage play, and activity.

Accessories: more or less $100 in total

If you bought a cage, you'll definitely need cage accessories like perches, lights, feeding dishes, stands, cage covers and harnesses for your Rose-ringed parrot. Accessories can be quite expensive depending on the brand as well as the quality of your purchase.

Toys: average total cost is $50

Rose-ringed parakeets like to chew things and needs plenty of stimulation to keep their intelligent and active minds entertained. Keep birdie boredom at bay with chewable toys for your ringneck.

Grooming Supplies: more or less $70 in total

As part of pet hygiene, your feathered friend needs to be cleaned and properly groomed. There are lots of grooming supplies that you can buy online or in your local pet store.

Initial Cost for Ringneck Parakeet	
Cost Type	**Approximate Cost**
Purchase Price	$100 (£88.86)
Cage	$170 (£151.06)
Accessories	$100 (£89)
Toys	$50 (£45)
Grooming Supplies	$70 (£63)
Total	$490 (£435.42)

*Please note that these amounts are computed at the starting price. Costs may vary.

b.) Monthly Costs

The monthly costs associated with keeping an Ringneck Parakeet can be quite expensive! Some of the things that needs to be bought on a monthly basis like food supplements, cleaning materials and even veterinary care every now and then will definitely add up to your expenses. Below are the estimate monthly costs it entails.

Bird Food (seeds, pellets, treats, fruits, vegetables, etc): approximately $40-$50 per month

Your Ringneck needs a varied and healthy diet. There's a massive selection of high quality seed diets, complete food and pelleted foods to choose from both online and in your local pet stores, as mentioned before, the cost will depend on the brand as well as the nutritional value of the food.

Feeding a variety of these foods, alongside fruits and vegetables is the key to a healthy parrot.

Cleaning Supplies: at least $10 per month

You don't need brand new cleaning supplies every month, but of course, you will run out of bird shampoo and soap eventually. Just include it in your budget.

Veterinary Care. starts at $150 - $1,000 or more

Take your Ringneck Parakeet to an avian vet for any medical check-up every now and then. Avian vets are trained specifically to work with exotic birds whereas a general practicing vet may not be familiar with their needs and treatments especially if they are sick, not to mention the medicines needed.

Additional Costs: at least $10 per month

In addition to all of these monthly costs you should plan for occasional extra costs like repairs to your parakeet's cage, replacement toys, food supplements, medicines etc. You won't have to cover these costs every month but you should include it in your budget to be safe.

Monthly Costs for Ringneck Parakeets	
Cost Type	Approximate Cost
Bird Food	$40 (£35.54)
Cleaning Supplies	$10 (£8)
Veterinary Care (optional)	$150 (£135)
Additional Costs	$10 (£8)
Total	$210 (£186.61)

*Please note that these amounts are computed at the starting price. Costs may vary.

Chapter Four: Tips in Buying Ringneck Parakeets

If you are still interested in reading this chapter, that only means one thing: you have already decided to buy a Ringneck Parakeet! Great choice! They are ideal as a first pet.

Here you will learn tips and tricks on how to select a healthy Ringneck, where to find the right breeder as well as the laws and permit you need to be aware of before buying.

1.) Restrictions and Regulations in United States

If you are planning to acquire a Ringneck Parakeet as your pet, then you have to think beyond the cage. There are certain restrictions and regulations that you need to be aware of, because it will not only serve as protection for your bird but also for you. Here are some things you need to know regarding the acquirement of Ringneck Parakeet both in United States and in Great Britain.

a.) Legal Reminder

The Ringneck Parakeet must be banded as prescribed by law. Banding enables you to track the individual identification of the bird, its movement and history. This ensures that the bird you acquired is legal and not smuggled.

b.) What is CITES?

CITES stands for Convention on International Trade in Endangered Species of Wild Fauna and Flora. It protects Ringneck Parakeets by regulating its import, export, and re-export through an international convention authorized through a licensing system.

It is also an international agreement, drafted by the International Union for Conservation of Nature (IUCN), which aims to ensure that the trade in specimens of wild animals and plants does not threaten their survival.

Different species are assigned in different appendix statuses such as Appendix I, II or III etc. These appendices indicate the level of threat to the current population of the bird with consideration to their likely ability to rebound in the wild with legal trade.

One of the advantages of the Ringneck Parakeet is that it is NOT listed in CITES appendices, which simply means that **it does not require CITES permits.** Yes, you can travel with your Ringneck as much as you want without any restrictions, provided that you'll take care of them and not lose them.

2.) Permit in Great Britain and Australia

In Great Britain and Australia you may need a permit for you to be able to import, export, or travel with your Ringneck Parakeet. This permit is called an **Animal Movement License**. It is required for the prevention of the spread of communicable diseases.

In U.K. you can also get a license if you are looking to kill or catch a wild bird solely for the prevention of serious damage to your land or crops and to also prevent the spread of serious diseases. For more information on how to get a license to kill or catch a wild bird, you can visit their website:

<https://www.gov.uk/government/publications/wild-birds-licence-to-take-or-kill-to-prevent-damage-or-disease>

Like in the United States being aware of the regulations and getting a license is an important thing you need to consider before you acquire, import or export a bird. This does not only protect the animals but it can also avoid confiscation of your pet.

3.) Practical Tips in Buying Ringneck Parakeet

Now that you are already aware and have prior knowledge about the legal aspects of owning a Rose-ringed parrot, the next step is purchasing one through a local pet store or a legitimate breeder.

Here are some recommendations for finding a reputable Ringneck or Rose-ringed Parakeet breeder in United States and in Great Britain.

a.) How to Find a Ringneck Parakeet Breeder

The first thing you need to do is to look for a legit avian breeder or pet store in your area that specializes in Ringneck Parakeets.

You can also find great avian breeders online but you have to take into consideration the validity of the breeder. It is highly recommended that you see your new bird in person before buying anything on the internet. You can find several recommended list of Ringneck breeder websites later in this book.

Spend as much time as you can with your prospective new Ringneck parakeet before buying it. Interact with the bird and see how it is with you.

Continue the diet of the bird as advised by the store owner or breeder to maintain its eating habits. Look for any health problems or issues as well.

Finally, only purchase a Ringneck Parakeet that is banded. Banding means the bird have a small metal band on one of its legs placed at birth by the breeder which is inscribed with the bird's clutch number, date of birth and the breeder number.

Leg bands are indicators that the purchaser and the bird itself are in the country legally and have not been smuggled.

b.) Ringneck Parakeet Breeders in the United States

Here are the lists of Ringneck Parakeet breeders in the United States sorted by state.

If you don't find anyone near you, contact the closest one to your location and ask for a referral or a lead of the trusted breeders.

Alabama
Admirable Birds

Alabama, Estill Fork: Tel. (256) 776-2120

Remarks: Does not ship; delivers within 200 miles of Huntsville, Alabama

California
Steven Garvin - The Feather Tree - www.feathert.com

P.O. Box 8401 Long Beach, CA 90808 - Tel. (562) 429-1892

Remarks: Free educational DVD with each pet bird. Please refer to www.feathert.com for availability, photos and pricing. They ships nationally.

Maggie Maguire

Yreka, CA

Tel No.: (530) 841-0286

Colorado

Rocky Mtn. Bird Farm and Pet Supply

www.parrots4ever.com

E-mail: www.rockymtnbirdfarm@hotmail.com

Monument, Colorado

Phone 719-466-3310 or 805-503-9592 - Fax 719-481-8273

Avalon Aviary Bird Store

6014 W US Hwy 34, Loveland, CO 80537,

www.avalonaviary.com

E-mail: avalonstore@frii.com

Tel. 970 663-5004,

Remarks: MAP-certified breeder

Florida

Ziggy's Avian Ranch

Hudson, FL

E-mail: bob.susan@verizon.net

Tel. 727-819-9839

Remarks: Will ship or drive 1/2 way in Florida.

Shady Pines Aviary

Royal Palm Beach, FL
Gloria Balaban
Tel. 352-454-4208

Jean (The African Queen) Pattison
New Tampa Highway, Lakeland, Florida 33815 U.S.A.
Phone: 863-686-4532
E-mail: afqueen@gate.net

Indiana
Royal Wings Aviary
www.royalwingsaviary.com.
Contact: Allan or Pam at (574) 273-1767
E-mail: pam@royalwingsaviary.com

Iowa
Zimmerman Pet's
N.W Iowa (Sioux City, IA).
Tel. 712-239-5531

New York
MY Lovely Doves and Etc.
Middletown NY 10940
E-mail: sheree@citlink.net
Tel: 845-341-0411

North Carolina

Avian Paradise - www.AvianParadise.com

Kernersville, North Carolina

Ohio

Parrotville Bird Shop, Brunswick

Oh 44212

www.parrotville.com

Tel. 330-273-0100

Oregon

The Parrot Patch Aviary

Eugene, Oregon

Tel. 541-463-9564

Karol and Jerry Fredrickson

Grants Pass, OR

Tel No.: 955-8946

Bev Bravo

Grants Pass, OR

Tel No.: (541) 862-2097

Sharon Holscher

White City, OR

Tel No.: (541) 826-8687

South Dakota
Feather Focus

www.featherfocus.com

E-mail: personal@featherfocus.com

Texas
SpringOak

Mailing Address: P.O. Box 231, Dripping Springs TX 78620

Tel. 512-630-1626

E-mail: Donray1953@msn.com

Utah
KCZAR Aviaries - www.kczaraviaries.com

Ogden, Utah

Tel. 801-731-5166

Virginia
Sissy Crawford - Sissy's Bird Colony

Aylett, Virginia

www.sissysbirdcolony.com

Washington
Jades Jungle Love

Arlington, Washington.

Tel. 425 238-4822

c.) Ringneck Parakeet Breeders in Great Britain

Here are the links and contact details of Ringneck Parakeet breeders in Great Britain:

Local Breeders

Mark Jones
South Wales
Email: jones-jonathan@tiscali.co.uk

Wayne Kemble
Swindon, England
Email: waynekemble@yahoo.co.uk
Tel No.: 01793 490107

Roy Talbot
Email: roy.talbot@ntlworld.com

UK Breeder Websites

Barrett Watson Parrots
<http://www.barrettwatsonparrots.co.uk>

Hand Reared Parrots
<http://www.handrearedparrots.co.uk/>

Xotic Birds

<http://www.xoticbirds.co.uk/>

Bird Trader

<http://www.birdtrader.co.uk/>

4.) Selecting a Healthy Ringneck Parakeet

Ringneck Parakeet can live for up to 30 years and more, these birds are long time companions, and its longevity depends on how your chosen breeders took care of them especially when they were young.

This section will give you simple tips on how you can spot a healthy Ringneck that you can keep for life!

a.) Signs of a Healthy Bird

Look out for these signs so that you know if your prospect bird is healthy:

- The bird should be active, alert, and sociable
- It should eat and drink throughout the day
- It should have dry nostrils and bright, dry eyes
- The beak, legs, and feet should have normal appearance
- It should have a dry and clean vent
- Its feathers should be smooth and well-groomed

Chapter Five: Caring Guidelines for Ringneck Parakeets

Assuming that you have already bought a Ringneck Parakeet as your pet, the responsibility that comes with it is the most crucial part of the process. You as the owner, have to provide for its basic needs so that it will be healthy and happy. In this chapter you will learn the requirements your bird needs for its cage, diet and what accessories is best for your Ringneck parakeet.

1.) Habitat and Environment

Ringneck Parakeets have adapted well to human-modified habitats, such as parks and gardens in villages and towns. Like other kinds of birds, Ringneck Parakeets should be kept in a bird-safe environment. As the owner you need to have knowledge of its habitat requirements and environmental conditions to ensure that your bird is healthy. You will find tons of information in this section regarding the requirements your pet needs in order to keep them happy.

a.) Ideal Cage Size for Ringneck Parakeets

A relatively tall iron cage, suited for their long tails is the best home for a Rose-ringed parakeet. The ideal size of a cage for a Rose-ringed parakeet is 24 inches wide by 18 inches deep by 36 inches high (60 x 45 x 90 cm).

It is ideal that the cage material uses nontoxic paint or else it can cause your pet to be poisoned by metal. It shouldn't also be made out of brass because it contains zinc which could kill your parrot as well.

Ideally the cage should also have at least three doors. One as the main entrance and the other two should be used for food and water.

Your bird will be spending most of their lives inside the cage that's why it needs to be large so that it can also accommodate lots of toys and perches. The basic rule of thumb is - the bigger the better!

The spacing between the bars of the cage should be between 1.25 cm (1/2 inch) and 1.875 cm (3/4 inch). If the bars are too far apart, your parakeet might try to squeeze through them and sneak out because they just love to fly and be free! You don't want to lose them right?

A great factor to determine the perfect cage for your parrot, is that it should be big enough to do all of their "stunts" such as flapping its wings, going from one perch to another, and being able to relax comfortably without touching the bars of the cage. Ringnecks loves cages with lots of space and will make use of any excess room they have for sure.

b.) Cage Maintenance

Your parrot's cage could affect the health of your pet so it's very important that you check it daily for any dirt, like the feces and spoiling food left in perches and cups to prevent health problems.

You should also change the cage paper every other day as well as check the metal parts & bars of your bird's cage periodically for chipped paint and rust, because your bird will most likely chew or swallow the flaked pieces. You should be able to clean the cage thoroughly at least once every month. You could use a mild dishwashing liquid or bleach with warm water for about 1 minute. Then rinse all soap and bleach thoroughly with water before letting your bird inside the cage.

c.) Location of the Cage

Finding the perfect cage is just as important as knowing where to place it. The cage should be placed in a location where it is relatively quiet and they will not be disturbed with unnecessary noise.

If you find your ringneck having a hard time coping with its new environment, then a quiet place to relax is highly recommended so that it could get acquainted with its surroundings.

Put the cage at an eye level to create a sense of confidence in your bird and place the cage in a higher location so that they would feel secure just like in the wild.

Avoid placing the cage in a window because the sun can cause your parrot to become ill because of too much heat. Find the right balance between the sunlight and an appropriate amount of shade for your parakeet.

Finding the right location of the cage could lessen stressful situations for your bird so that they can enjoy their life with their new owner.

d.) Recommended Supplies

Now that your cage is all set, you need to provide supplies to meet its needs. Here are the recommended supplies that your Ringneck Parakeet needs:

Perches

It is ideal that you have different sizes of perches otherwise your bird's feet will not be properly exercised. This could also prevent sores and foot related health issues. You'll also need at least 3 different types of perches such as wood dowel, natural branch type, a therapeutic perch or a cement perch as well as Eucalyptus branches, just make sure that it is not poisonous. These perches could be used as ropes and swings for your pet. Keep in mind that anything you put inside the cage will be chewed. Do not also put the perch above the bird's bowl or dishes otherwise the food and water will be contaminated.

Seeds, Pellet, Fruits and Vegetables

Some Ringneck owners feed their birds only with seeds, while some only provides a pellet diet; this however could limit the nutrients your pet is receiving. Experts suggest that parrots should be given a variety of food for a balanced nutrition. These kind of parrots tend to have a good appetite, most Ringnecks will devour fruits and vegetables as well as seeds, they can easily be converted to a healthy diet if you provide them with all this nutrition.

You will need a good supply of packaged pellet dict, to be mixed with seed. Then you can slowly add fresh foods and other vitamins needed. Conversion takes about a week or so depending on your bird and how well you feed them.

Treats

Ringnecks love to do tricks once you trained them, and it always comes with a price! You can give your pet different types of treats such as fruits, seed and spray as well as Do-It-Yourself (DIY) treats like pretzels, popcorn or something healthy that your bird can munch on. Later in this book, you will be provided with a list of recommended treats as well as treats you should avoid.

Protein

In the wild, some Ringnecks eat insects for protein. In captivity you could provide them with a shred of cooked chicken or turkey meat.

Toys

Ringnecks are playful creatures, and like humans they need to have fun once in a while to prevent boredom and keep them happy. You should purchase at least 3 different toys because this will allow you to interchange them. Do not put all of the toys inside your bird's cage.

Otherwise it will become dirty and overcrowded. Rotate the toys at least once a week.

Dishes

Buy at least 3 sturdy dishes; one for fresh water, one for pellet or seed mix and one for fresh foods.

e.) Grooming and Hygiene

Here are some things you need to know on how to maintain your bird's hygiene and keep a healthy life.

Provide a misting bottle or a birdbath. All birds should be gently misted with a water bottle at room temperature. The spray should be sprayed up over the bird much like a shower rain, never spray the bird directly in its face.

It's important that you keep an eye in your bird while it is bathing. Bathe your Ringneck with clean water. Distilled water is sometimes required. Speak to your veterinarian on the best choice of water for your bird. During its misting and bathing procedures, make sure there are no drafts because it can cause respiratory issues. It may chill your bird when he is wet. Use towels and blankets, but be careful because it can catch the bird's nails and beaks in their threads.

To ensure that the oils from their skin glands, disease organisms or items such as lotions and hand creams do not transfer to your bird's feathers, wash your hands with soap and water thoroughly before handling your Ringneck.

Your bird may be ill if it seems to stop grooming and becomes dirty. Once you see this signs, contact your avian veterinarian immediately.

f.) Lighting and Temperature

The average room temperature for your bird should not exceed 80 degrees. Avoid drafty areas that will get direct heat from sun for any portion of the day.

Parrots also have tetra-chromic vision (4 color light vision including ultraviolet), that's why a full color light bulb must be present in the cage area. The incandescent or monochromatic light bulbs usually found in households are not a good choice for your parakeet.

Cover the cage during nighttime; it blocks out any excess light and also creates a more secure sleeping place. Be careful when using fabrics as cover because your bird might rip it with its claws or beak and could likely eat it.

Never ever place the cage in the kitchen or somewhere near cooking fumes because parakeets are very sensitive, that even a small amount of smoke can be fatal.

2.) *Diet and Feeding*

      Ringneck Parakeets are largely considered herbivorous, they feed off on nuts, seeds, fruits and vegetables and some insects on occasion. Its food preferences are mostly based on its natural habitat. Thankfully, today's supplements have opened new and healthy options for pet owners. In this section you will be guided on how to properly feed your parrot and learn the nutritional requirements they need.

a.) Nutritional Needs of Ringneck Parakeets

Feeding your Rose-ringed parakeet is not that complicated. Usually in the wild, these birds devour fruits nuts, vegetables, seeds and pretty much anything that is edible in the surroundings around them. They're not choosy eaters but like what was mentioned earlier, it is highly recommended that parrots should be given a variety of food for a balanced nutrition.

As much as possible avoid only giving the same type of food such as a pellet diet or seed diet only; it can result in nutrient deficiency and diseases due to its limited nutrients, which could shorten the life expectancy of your parrot.

This section outlines the foods your pet will appreciate in order to meet the majority of its dietary needs.

b.) Types of Food

Seeds and Pellet

Seeds are a big part of any bird's diet; they eat seeds naturally in the wild and it is also a good source of Carbohydrates. However, seeds alone can cause complications because it is naturally fatty. It is not advisable that you mixed seeds with pellets, offer seeds first for a few days, then slowly offer pellets as well until your Ringneck learns how to eat it because some Ringnecks don't know how to eat pellets.

The key is to give it in moderation. Feed them at least 3-4 teaspoons per day of a pellet or seed-based, fortified parrot diet.

Fresh Vegetables

Vegetables are a rich source of natural fiber for the body, because it does not only provide fiber but also nutrition. However, keep in mind that you should feed them with vegetables in moderation to prevent diarrhea and make sure they are properly washed before feeding it to your bird.

Below is the list of highly recommended vegetables for Ringneck Parakeets:

- Artichoke
- Asparagus
- Beets and greens
- Broccoli and greens
- Cabbage
- Carrots
- Cauliflower and greens
- Celery
- Chard
- Chickweed
- Chicory
- Chinese Cabbage
- Cucumber

- Dandelion Greens
- Edamame
- Eggplant
- Fennel and leaves, stems, seeds
- Kale
- Leeks
- Lettuce (darker is better)
- Mustard Greens
- Okra
- Peas/Snap Peas/String Beans/Snow Peas
- Peppers (all types)
- Radicchio
- Radish and greens
- Spinach
- Sweet Potato/Yam (cooked/parboiled)
- Squash (all types)
- Tomatoes (offer in moderation)
- Turnips and turnip greens
- Watercress
- Wheat Grass
- Yams

Fruits

Fruits are healthy and sweet, they are natural sources of sugars for the parrots. It is recommended that you only offer a bite-sized fruits and also remove the pits or seeds of the fruits to prevent choking.

Below are list of fruits that are highly recommended by veterinarians for your Rose-ringed parrot:

- Apples (no seed)
- Apricots (no seed)
- Banana
- Blackberries
- Blueberries
- Cherries (no seed)
- Coconut (feed sparingly due to fat content)
- Cranberries
- Custard Apple
- Dragon Fruit
- Figs
- Guava
- Grapefruit
- Grapes
- Kiwi Fruit
- Lemon
- Lime
- Longan
- Lychee
- Mango (no seed)
- Melon (cantaloupe, watermelon, honeydew)

- Nectarinc (no seed)
- Olive (fresh)
- Oranges
- Papaya
- Passion Fruit
- Peach (no seed)
- Pear (no seed)
- Pineapple
- Plum (no seed)
- Pomegranate
- Pomelo
- Quince
- Raspberries
- Rose Hips
- Rowan Berries
- Schizandra Berries
- Starfruit
- Strawberries
- Tamarillo
- Tangerine

Important Reminder:

Offer fruits and vegetables daily or every 2-3 days. As a caution, if your parakeet didn't consume all the fruits you gave, remove all of its traces from the cage to avoid the risk of eating a spoiled fruit.

Grains

Grains are also part of a healthy bird's diet; however it is very important that you only feed your bird with small amounts so that they could digest it properly.

Below are some of the recommended kinds of grains that you should feed to your pet:

- Brown Rice (recommended with cooked beans)
- Buckwheat
- Corn (whole kernel; frozen/fresh/dried/cooked: cob, plumped, popped, cracked)
- Hemp
- Oat Groat/Hulled Oat
- Oatmeal
- Pasta
- Pearl Barley
- Quinoa

Protein

Proteins are amino acids which are building blocks of life that is why your ringneck also needs a good amount of protein to keep them healthy. As mentioned before, parakeets get their protein through feeding off insects in the wild. Fortunately, you don't have to get insects to provide protein for your bird!

Here is the list of recommended protein for your pet Ringneck to feed on:

- Beans (cook small amounts as needed)
- Chicken (cooked, preferably shredded)
- Eggs (cooked/hard boiled)
- Nuts (all types)
- Peanuts
- Seeds (birdseeds provide protein)
- Sprouts
- Turkey (cooked, preferably shredded)
- Yoghurt (yes, you read that right!)

Supplements

The only supplement necessary in feeding your parrot is Calcium. Calcium is usually found in the form of a cuttlebone or Calcium treat that is attached inside your bird cage. You can also offer a powdered supplement such as packaged oyster shell which can be added directly to your pet's food. Follow the instructions on the supplement package. Calcium is vital for muscle contraction, blood clotting, heart functions, bone growth and strength.

The bird should be exposed to UVB light for at least 3-4 hours a day, for optimal physiologic use of the calcium you are giving your bird.

Herbs and Spices

In addition to the types of food mentioned above, you can also feed your Ringneck parakeets with herbs and spices that can be easily available to your home. As always, feed them in moderation.

Here are recommended herbs you might want to feed to your pet bird:

- Alfalfa
- Aloe
- Basil
- Bay leaf
- Chives
- Cinnamon (Ceylon)
- Garlic
- Ginger Root
- Lemon balm
- Lemongrass
- Mint
- Oregano
- Paprika
- Parsley
- Rosemary
- Thyme
- Turmeric

Water

Hydration is just as important for birds as it is for human beings especially during hot weather conditions, lack of water can lead to dehydration which can cause these birds to collapse. Your Rose-ringed Parakeets should be given access to clean, fresh and cool water. Do not use tap water because can cause the bird to be ill, as well as distilled water, instead use unflavored bottled drinking water or bottled natural spring water. If in case, tap water is used, treat it with a de-chlorinating treatment. Inability to provide fresh water to pet birds can cause upset stomach with unbearable stomachache.

Whether the meal consists of raw or cooked food, vegetables or meat Rose-ringed Parakeets have a habit of drinking water after every meal which helps their digestion process.

All water given to birds for drinking, as well as water used for misting, soaking or bathing must be 100% free of chlorine and heavy metals.

Treats

As mentioned earlier, you could give your parrots a reward every time they do something right like performing tricks or simply behaving during training. You can feed them with bite-sized fruits and seeds as well as DIY (Do-It-Yourself) treats.

Some examples of DIY treats are carrot muffins (minus the sugar), popcorn, corn, unsalted pretzel sticks with fruits and brown rice with berries. They will surely love something appetizing to eat and this is also a positive reinforcement for the bird especially during training them.

c.) Toxic Foods to Avoid

Some foods are specifically toxic for your Rose-ringed Parakeet. Make sure that your bird never gets to eat one of the toxic items below and ensure that an avian veterinary checks your bird every now and then. These harmful foods is as important as selecting the right supplements and food items for your bird.

The following list of foods is toxic for your Rose-ringed Parakeet:

- Chocolate (highly allergic)
- Avocados
- Junk Food
- Apple and Cherry Seeds
- Lettuce
- Milk and Dairy Products

3.) Handling and Training Ringneck Parakeets

There would be instances that your pet will be out of its cage; after all, what's the point of its beauty and intelligence if you won't let it fly right? However, it's also important to keep in mind on how to properly handle and train your bird so that it will not cause harm to itself and to people as well.

In this section, you'll learn some guidelines on how to confidently handle your parrot as well as some tips on trimming its nails and wings to maximize its balance and flying potential.

a. Tips for Training Your Ringneck Parakeet

Training a Rose-ringed Parakeet is not that hard to do, in fact it can be a fun and rewarding bonding experience for you and your feathered friend! Ringneck Parakeets are one of the most intelligent birds in history; they can absorb information very quickly and easily as long as you do it right.

Trust is the most important key in training your parrot. The first thing you need to do is to be able to establish a solid connection and rapport between you and your pet.

This section will provide some guidelines you can follow in getting your bird well behaved and disciplined. Are you ready? Read on!

Stepping Up is a basic skill your parrot should learn, to find out how to do this follow the tips below:

- A good way to pacify your bird into your hands without being forceful is to try and make your parakeet step up onto a handheld perch.
- Slowly and progressively begin training it to step up on your hand. If you are afraid of being bitten then wear gloves, but you may want to get rid of it eventually because it might still encourage them to bite you because they can chew the leather.
- Hold your hand in a short distance away from your parrot so that when it tries to step into the target stick, it will have no choice but to step into your hand.
- Keep practicing until your parrot won't need your stick anymore. It will get accustomed and comfortable whenever you command it to step up in your finger

b.) Tips for Taming Your Ringneck Parakeet

Once you have achieved some basic skills with your Ringneck, the next thing to do is to tame them.

The flipside of owning a Ringneck parakeet is that they quite an attitude and also known as a biter. The key is to figure out the level of your bird's comfort zone and remove it so that you could have a great bonding experience together. Here are some tips on how to do tame your Ringneck parakeet:

- Start by slowly touching your parrot in its beak. Carefully move your hand closer and closer towards its beak. If the parrot reacts or moves away, stop for a while.
- Wait for it to calm down, then take your hand away and give a treat.
- Practices repeating this procedure until you are able to fully touch its beak. Your ringneck will eventually tolerate you in touching its beak and once you do, you can also scratch their beak. They like that.

c.) Trimming Your Ringneck Parakeet Nails

Like many parrots, Ringneck Parakeets have a very sharp, needle-like nails because they do a lot of climbing in the wild, and they also use these nails to dig into wood to keep them secure.

Unclipped nails can dig into the skin, leaving scratches or painful wounds to a person, only clipped to a point that the bird can perch securely and does not bother you when the bird is perched on your hand. Many people have their Ringneck's nails clipped to the point that it becomes dull and the bird can no longer grip a perch firmly. This can result to becoming more clumsy and nervous because it cannot move without slipping. This nervousness can develop into fear biting and panic attacks.

Another tip is only use a styptic powder on your bird's nails, not the skin!

d.) Clipping a Ringneck Parakeet Wings

Birds are design to fly, young ringneck parakeets can be fairly clumsy and flying gives them confidence as well as agility, stamina, and muscle tone.

Before clipping their wings, make sure that your parakeets are flying, maneuvering and landing well already. If they do not learn how to properly land by lifting their wings and flaring their tail, then when they are clipped, they could injure themselves and could also break their beak or keel bone.

Consult a qualified veterinarian to show you the proper way in clipping a bird's wings. A certain amount of flight feathers will be removed while leaving the smaller balancing feathers inside the wing closer to the body uncut.

Chapter Six: Breeding Ringneck Parakeets

If you decided to buy two Ringneck Parakeets, for instance a male and female and keep them together, you should definitely prepare for the possibility of breeding, unless it's the same gender, otherwise you're going to be caught off guard!

If you are interested in breeding your Ringneck Parakeets this chapter will give you a wealth of information about the processes and phases of its breeding and you will also learn how to properly breed them on your own. This is not for everyone but if you want to have better understanding about how these birds procreate, then you should definitely not miss this part! On the contrary if you are interested in becoming a reputable breeder, then this is a must read chapter for you.

1.) Basic Ringneck Parakeet Breeding Info

Before deciding if you truly want to become a breeder, you should at least have prior knowledge on their basic reproduction process and breeding. This section will inform you on how these creatures procreate.

a.) Sexual Dimorphism

Ringnecks are sexually dimorphic, males and females are quite easy to distinguish visually because of the color bands around their neck. Males have an obvious black ring while females' rings are not that prominent, although if you look closely around their neck, you can see that one is paler green than their body color.

You can also determine the gender of your bird through DNA analysis, which uses sample blood or feathers; it can also provide additional information on its sexual maturity and capability to reproduce. It is inexpensive and convenient so if you like to know more about your bird's sexuality you should definitely try DNA Sexing or Surgical Sexing.

b.) Mating and Reproduction

In the wild, Ringnecks breed in single pairs and mates in colonies with 8 to 9 couples inside the cavities of a tree. The sexual maturity of Ringneck parakeet happens between 5 to 36 months. You'll need to provide a nesting box because that is where females will lay their eggs.

The breeding period starts at earliest in February and ends in July. Generally, females lays about 3 or 5 eggs per clutch on alternate days and incubation takes approximately 22-24 days. During the incubation period, females rarely leave the nest while the male takes on the responsibility of feeding her and the chicks.

It is highly recommended that you provide an additional 20% increase on fatty seeds as well as their intake of vitamin supplements and proteins such as hard-boiled egg and shredded chicken during the breeding process.

It's also important to note that the temperature should be kept between 12° - 18°C (55°- 65°F) and humidity needs to be raised to about 80% before the eggs are hatched.

2.) The Ringneck Parakeet Breeding Process

In order to have a clear sketch of a Rose-ringed parrot breeding, this section will show you the breeding process and the information you need to know, so that your pets can successfully procreate.

a.) Selecting Ringneck Parakeets for Breeding

For you to select a healthy, fertile and active parrot it is recommended that your parrot undergoes clinical examination by a veterinarian. This is essential to determine if your parrot is capable of reproduction or not and at the same time it can prevent diseases that could be transmitted to the coming flock.

b.) Setting up a Good Environment and Cage

As mentioned earlier, Ringneck Parakeets are naturally cavity dwellers in the wild. However, in captivity, you need to set up a nice environment for them so that they can successfully breed. The minimum cage size is 24in x 24in x 48in.; ideally 48 inches should be the depth and the front of the cage should be 24 in x 24 in preferably with feeding stations.

Set up an artificial nest or box and make sure it has an entrance hole of about 4" in diameter. You can also line the nest with a soft hand towel. It is also advisable to make some holes to the bottom of the box to allow drainage of excess water if in case you want to put it outside your house. You can also add some peat, wood chips, and small pieces of coconut fibers, foam, dry grass or hay to replicate a natural nest. Put your cage at a place where they will feel secure and where nobody will disturb them.

c.) Brooding and Incubation

Breeding time starts in February and ends in July. Only the female incubates and its clutch size ranges from

2-6, and there is a 1-2 days gap after laying the first egg. On average 3-4 eggs are laid, and incubation lasts for about 22 to 24 days.

d.) Hatching

The eggs hatch in about 24 days and it takes about 6 to 7 weeks before the young parakeets leave the nest. After leaving the nest, chicks are still being fed by their parents and in approximately 2 weeks after that, the parents' starts to separate themselves from their babies and the chicks becomes independent.

Chapter Seven: Keeping Ringneck Parakeets Healthy

You as the owner should be aware of the potential threats and diseases that could harm the wellness of your Ringneck Parakeet. Just like human beings, you need to have knowledge on these diseases so that you can prevent it from happening in the first place. You will find tons of information on the most common problems that may affect your bird including its causes, signs and symptoms, remedies and prevention.

1.) Common Health Problems

In this section, you will learn about the diseases that may affect and threaten your parakeet's wellness. Learning these diseases as well as its remedies is vital for you and your bird so that you could prevent it from happening or even help with its treatment in case they caught one.

Below are some of the most common health problems that occur specifically to Rose-ringed parrots. You will learn some guidelines on how these diseases can be prevented and treated as well as its signs and symptoms.

Psittacosis or Parrot Fever

It is a zoonotic infectious disease caused by an unknown organism whose natural host is *psittacine* birds.

a.) Cause and Effect

It is an airborne disease and it can also be spread via the bird's feces. This disease is highly contagious. Before acquiring a Ringneck Parakeet, it's important that your bird goes through a Psittacosis test because this type of infection can also potentially harm a human being.

b.) Signs and Symptoms

The worst thing about this disease is that it is asymptomatic, which means symptoms does not appear or cannot be detected easily, you will never know when it could happen and if the bird is a carrier. Nevertheless, watch out for these possible signs that your pet might be having Psittacosis:

- Difficulty in breathing (due to Respiratory infections with airsac)
- Sneezing
- Runny eyes
- Congestion
- Liver disease might occur (and can progress rapidly to death)

c.) Diagnosis of Psittacosis

As mentioned earlier, this type of disease is asymptomatic that sometimes even a psittacosis test could not detect the disease. Identifying organisms in the feces is done in most cases.

d.) Treatment and Remedy

This disease is treated with a tetracycline based antibiotic given for about 45 days to eliminate the carrier state, although some veterinarians believe that the antibiotic does not necessarily remove the carrier state.

Pacheco's Disease

This disease is caused by a herpes virus which attacks the liver and results in acute liver failure. It is very contagious and highly fatal to most birds.

a.) Diagnosis

Diagnosis is done via necropsy which detects microscopic evidences of the virus found in the liver.

b.) Treatment and Remedy

Unfortunately, there is no guaranteed antibiotic or remedy for this disease, the best you could do is to minimize the spread of the virus through intensive care and some antiviral medication.

Aspergillosis

It is a respiratory disease caused by the fungus called *Aspergillus*, which is found in warm and moist environments.

a.) Cause and Effect

The microscopic spores of Aspergillus are an airborne transmitted disease. The fungus does not cause the disease per se but if your bird does not have a healthy immune system it can cause illness.

It increases the chances of the spores being inhaled by your bird if the environment has poor ventilation and sanitation, dusty conditions, and in close confinements.

Other predisposing factors include poor nutrition, other medical conditions in the respiratory system and prolonged use of antibiotics or corticosteroids, which eventually weakens the immune system. Aspergillosis is more common in parrots than other pet birds.

b.) Signs and Symptoms

There are two kinds of Aspergillosis, it's either acute or chronic, both of which attacks the respiratory system.

Acute Aspergillosis signs and symptoms include:

- Severe difficulty in breathing
- Cyanosis (a bluish coloration of mucous membranes and/or skin)
- Decreased or loss of appetite
- Frequent drinking and urination

Chronic Aspergillosis symptoms include:

- White nodules appear through the respiratory tissue
- Large numbers of spores enter the bloodstream
- Infection in the kidneys, skin, muscle, gastrointestinal

tract, liver, eyes, and brain

Other signs of Aspergillosis may include:

- Rapid breathing
- Exercise intolerance
- Change in syrinx (voice box); reluctance to talk
- Discharged and clogging of Nares
- Tremors
- Seizures or paralysis
- Green discoloration in the urates may be seen
- Enlarged liver
- Gout (painful, inflamed joints due to urate deposits)
- Depression and lethargy

c.) Diagnosis of Aspergillosis

Aspergillosis is generally difficult to detect until complete diagnosis. Do not compromise respiratory infections, consult the veterinarian immediately.
Here are some of the tests that your Ringneck needs to undergo through for diagnosis

- Radiographs (a complete blood count)
- Endoscopy (used to view lesions in the syrinx or trachea)
- PCR testing for the presence of Aspergillus

d.) Treatment and Remedy

Always consult a veterinarian first to know the right remedy for your bird. There are reports that the antifungal drug Itraconazole may be more toxic to Ringneck parrots than to other bird species. Another antifungal drug called Amphotericin B may be administered orally, topically, by injection, or nebulizing. Consult your vet for proper guidance. Surgery may also be performed to remove accessible lesions. Supportive care is often needed such as oxygen, supplemental heat, tube feeding, and treatment of underlying conditions.

e.) Prevention

Maintaining a good husbandry and diet can highly prevent outbreaks of Aspergillosis.

Below are some tips you can do to ensure that your bird is free from such a deadly disease:

- Keep your bird in a well-ventilated environment.
- Always clean the food and water dishes
- Thoroughly clean cages, toys, perches and other accessories at least once a month.
- Replace substrate (material lining the cage bottom) regularly
- Offer a good nutrition, such as the right combination of fruits, vegetables and seeds

Psittacine Beak and Feather Disease (PBFD)

PBFD is a viral condition that is responsible for damage to the beak, feathers and nails as well as the immune system of infected birds. These are very common in Ringneck parrots between 6 months and 3 years of age.

a.) Signs and symptoms

PBFD typically affects the feathers of infected birds as well as its beak and nails over time. Here are some signs and symptoms that your pet might have PBFD.

- Feathers are short, fragile, malformed, and prone to bleeding and breaking. Birds may first lose their the white, fine powder produced by specialized feathers to help maintain feather health when this happens more abnormal feathers will eventually develop.
- Beak has become glossy rather than the more typical matte appearance
- Nails and beak becomes brittle and malformed
- Significant loss of feathers (as the follicles become damaged)
- Loss of appetite (especially in young Ring-necks)
- Regurgitation or continuous vomiting

b.) Diagnosis

Veterinarians will likely perform a PCR test to confirm the diagnosis. This test uses advanced techniques to look for the virus' DNA.

Most of the time PCR only needs a blood sample, but your veterinarian may also need to take a swab from your bird's mouth and vent.

Other kinds of test may include:
- Complete blood count and a chemistry panel tests.
- DNA test for specifically for PBFD

c.) Treatment

The majority of clinically affected birds will die within a few months to a year because there are no antiviral drugs available to fight the virus. Your avian veterinarian can only help keep your bird comfortable because this condition is painful for the bird and it also allows secondary infections to take hold. Some birds may survive for a few months they will ultimately die from this disease.

d.) Prevention

The only thing breeders and pet owners can do to prevent this deadly virus is to take pro-active steps but since you can't help the birds mingle with other birds as they travel from wholesaler to retail pet distributors to your home the best solution is to have your bird examined by an avian veterinarian and allow diagnostic testing.

It is also wise to take your bird for a yearly exam to make sure it stays healthy. Yearly exams can catch small issues before they get worse.

2.) Signs of Possible Illnesses

For you to keep your Ringneck Parakeet healthy, you need to monitor them to ensure that they are in good condition, however there will come a time that your bird will get sick. Here are some early warning signs that your bird could be potentially ill.

- **Activity** – Is your bird sleeping when it normally does not? Or being quiet when it normally isn't? Is there a decreased in food and water intake or not being able to eat at all like before?
- **Droppings** (feces) - Are there any change in urates (white part) or feces that is lasting more than 1-2 days?
- **Diarrhea** - Have you found undigested food in your bird's feces? Their droppings should have the three distinct parts (green/brown, white and liquid urine). If you think your parakeet has diarrhea, contact your vet immediately.

- **Weight loss** - Does your bird feels "light" when you pick it up? That maybe a sign of weight loss because the Keel bone becomes more prominent.
- **Feathers** – Is there a continuous presence of pinfeathers? It may be dull in color, broken, bent and fluffed up feathers.
- **Sneezing** – Is there a discharge in the nostrils when your bird sneezes? Look for stained feathers over the nares or crusty material in or around the nostrils.
- **Vomiting** – Has your pet been vomiting for quite a long period of time already? Parakeets and all birds regurgitate as a sign of "affection" but it could also indicate a crop infection
- **Respiratory** – Are there signs of respiratory distress like tail bobbing up and down with each breath, a change in breathing sounds, and wheezing or clicking noise when it inhales?
- **Balance** – Has your bird been falling off its perch and huddling at the bottom of cage? It is a sign that it's losing its balance.
- **Eyes** – Does it appear dull? Is there a redness/swelling and loss of feathers around the eyes?
- **Feet** – Is it scaly or flaky? Does it have sores on the bottom of the feet?

- **Head** – Have you noticed excessive head bobbing and

shaking?

- **Beak** – Is your bird's beak swelling?
- **Behavior** – does your bird sits on the floor of its cage or habitat? Does it favor one foot over the other?

When these things happen, contact your avian veterinarian immediately. Do not compromise your bird's health; prevention is always better than cure.

Chapter Eight: Ringneck Parakeet Checklist

Congratulate yourself! You are now on your way to becoming a very well-informed and pro-active Ringneck Parakeet owner! Finishing this book is a huge milestone for you and your future or present pet bird, but before this ultimate guide comes to a conclusion, keep in mind the most important things you have acquired through reading this book.

This chapter will outline the summary of what you have learned, the do's and dont's as well as the checklist you need to tick off to ensure that you and your Ringneck Parakeet lived happily ever after!

1.) Basic Information

- **Taxonomy**: phylum *Chordata*, class *Aves*, order *Psittaciformes*, family *Psittaculidae*, Genus *Psittacula*, Species *Psittacula krameri manillensis*
- **Distribution**: India, Sri Lanka, Africa, Asia
- **Habitat**: Tropical; Terrestrial
- **Anatomical Adaptations**:
- **Eggs**: 2-6 on average but usually 3-4 eggs per season
- **Incubation Period**: 22 - 24 days
- **Average Size**: 16 - 18 inches from head to tail
- **Average Weight**: 115 –140 grams
- **Wingspan**: 15 – 17 cm
- **Feather Count**: 12
- **Coloration**: green, blue, yellow
- **Sexual Dimorphism**: Males distinctively has three bands of color or rings around their necks; Females sometimes have a very pale ring but do not have a colored band on their necks.
  Diet: vegetables, seeds, flowers, fruits.
- **Vocalization**: mimicry; choruses

- **Lifespan**: 23 years in the wild; 45 to 60 years in captivity

2.) Cage Set-up Guide

- **Minimum Cage Dimensions**: 24 inches wide by 18 inches deep by 36 inches high (60 x 45 x 90 cm) for single bird
- **Cage Shape**: the bigger, the better. Never purchase a round cage.
- **Minimum Height**: 36 inches (90 cm)
- **Bar Spacing**: 1.25 cm (1/2 inch) to 1.875 cm (3/4 inch)
- **Required Accessories**: food and water dishes, perches, grooming and cleaning materials, cuttlebone, toys
- **Food/Water Dish**: 3 sturdy dishes; one for fresh water, one for pellet/seed mix, and one for fresh foods.
- **Perches**: at least 3 different perches; wood dowel, natural branch type, a therapeutic perch or a cement perch as well as Eucalyptus branch
- **Recommended Toys**: rotate at least 3 different toys; rope toys, stainless steel bells, swings etc.
- **Bathing Materials**: misting bottle; bath tub
- **Nests Materials**: wooden box; artificial box
- **Recommended Temperature Range**: average temperature, it should not exceed 80 degrees.

- **Lighting:** full color light bulb must be present in the cage area

3.) Nutritional Information

- **Types of Recommended Food:**
- **Seeds:** 3-4 teaspoons per day
- **Fresh Fruits and Vegetables:** makes up about 15 to 30% of a Ringneck parakeet's diet. Offer fruits and vegetables daily or every 2-3 days.
- **Supplements:** Calcium usually found in the form of a cuttlebone or Calcium treat. Powdered supplement such as packaged oyster shell can be added directly to your pet's food.
- **Protein:** makes up about 20% of a Ringneck parakeet's diet
- **Carbohydrates:** makes up about 10% of a Ringneck parakeet's diet (nuts, seeds, corn etc.)
- **Grains:** makes up about 15% to 20% of a Ringneck parakeet's diet
- **Water:** clean, fresh and cool water; unflavored bottled drinking water or bottled natural spring water

4.) Breeding Information

- **Sexual Dimorphism**: They are sexually dimorphic; Males have an obvious black ring while females' rings are not that prominent.
- **Seasonal Changes**: breeding season usually begins in February and ends in July.
- **Sexual Maturity:** 5 to 36 months
- **Cage Size:** 24in x 24in x 48in during breeding period
- **Egg Laying**: female lays lay 3-4 eggs with a gap of 1-2 days
- **Clutch Size**: 2 to 6 eggs per clutch
- **Incubation Period**: 22-24 days
- **Hatching**: takes about 24 days to hatch

5.) Do's and Dont's

- Do keep them busy and happy;
- Do feed them a variety of nutritious food
- Do train them well to maximize their intelligence
- Do provide a clean and healthy environment
- Do give them time and commitment
- Do care for them when they feel ill
- Do provide plenty of toys inside the cage
- Do bond with them and let them out of the cage once in a while so that they can be exposed outside
- Do not use sandpaper covered perches or floor paper. It can cause severe damage to your bird's feet

- Do not use "bird disks" or "mite disks". These may harm your bird. See your avian veterinarian if you suspect parasites.
- Do not use bird gravel. Bird gravel is used for birds that do not crack the hull or shell of the seeds they eat. It causes severe impactions, which are often fatal. Gravel only benefits doves and pigeons definitely not parrots
- Do not use negative reinforcement during training because it is not effective
- Don't let Ringneck Parakeets fall. It may contribute in developing respiratory problems and damages organs due to impact. Train them how to fly instead!

Chapter Nine: Relevant Websites

Finishing this book doesn't mean that you should stop learning! This chapter provides you a wealth of references online that you could check out every now and then so that you can be updated when it comes to taking care of your Ringneck Parakeet. You can also find the websites you need to visit especially in buying cages and supplies for your pet.

1. Ringneck Parakeet Cage Links

Here is the recommended list of websites for you to choose from when buying cages both in United States and Great Britain.

United States Links:

Cages by Design

<https://www.customcages.com/parakeet-cage.html>

Bird Cages 4 Less

<http://birdcages4less.com/page/B/CTGY/Parakeet-Budgie-Bird-Cages>

Bird Cages Now

<http://www.birdcagesnow.com/parakeets/>

King's Cages

<http://www.kingscages.com/SearchResults.aspx?SubCatID=Canary,%20Finch,%20Parakeet,%20Sugar%20Glider%20Cages>

Pet Solutions

<http://www.petsolutions.com/C/Small-Bird-Cages-Canaries-Finches-Parakeets+SAll.aspx>

Great Britain Links:

Cages World

<http://www.cagesworld.co.uk/f/Parrot_Cages/products::bird_type:Parakeet.htm >

Northern Parrots

<http://www.northernparrots.com/>

Pebble – Home and Garden

<https://www.pebble.co.uk/compare.html?q=Parakeet>

Seapets

<https://www.seapets.co.uk/bird-supplies/bird-cages/parrot-cages>

2. Ringneck Parakeet Cage Accessories

Here is the recommended list of websites for you to choose from when buying accessories such as toys, perches, dishes and other necessary supplies for your pet.

United States Links:

Doctors Foster and Smith – Toys, Accessories

<http://www.drsfostersmith.com/bird-supplies/bird-toys/parakeet-to-conure-toys/ps/c/5059/5648/5752>

Fun Time Birdy - Toys

<http://www.funtimebirdy.com/mediumbirdtoys.html>

Pet Mountain – Accessories

<http://www.petmountain.com/category/1013/1/parakeet-cage-accessories.html>

PetSmart – Bowls, Feeders
<http://www.petsmart.com/bird/bowls-feeders/cat-36-catid-400014>

Wind City Parrot - Accessories

<http://www.windycityparrot.com/All_c_711.html>

Great Britain Links:

Cages World - Accessories

<http://www.cagesworld.co.uk/c/Bird_Cage_Accessories.ht
m>

Parrot Essentials - Accessories

<http://www.parrotessentials.co.uk/>

Parrotize UK – Parrot Stands and Covers

<http://parrotize.co.uk/products/parrot-stands/>

Seapets – Bird Toys

<https://www.seapets.co.uk/bird-supplies/bird-toys>

ZooPlus – Accessories

<http://www.zooplus.co.uk/shop/birds/cage_accessories>

3. *Ringneck Parakeet Diet and Food Links*

Here is the recommended list of websites for you to choose from when buying seeds and parrot food for your pet.

United States Links:

Harrison's Bird Food

<http://www.harrisonsbirdfoods.com/>

Nature Chest - Bird Food

<http://www.naturechest.com/bifoforinri.html>

Petco – Bird Food; Treats

<http://www.petco.com/shop/en/petcostore/bird/bird-food-and-treats>

Pet Supplies Plus

<http://www.petsuppliesplus.com/thumbnail/Bird/Food-Treats/c/2142/2162.uts>

That Pet Place – Bird Food Supplies

<http://www.thatpetplace.com/bird-supplies/bird-food#!bird-food>

Great Britain Links:

Parrot Essentials UK – Vitamins and Minerals for birds

<http://www.parrotessentials.co.uk/vitamins-minerals/>

Scarletts Parrot Essentials UK - Parakeets feeds

<https://www.scarlettsparrotessentials.co.uk/catalogsearch/advanced/result/?name=Parakeet&x=0&y=0>

Seapets – Bird Food

<https://www.seapets.co.uk/bird-supplies/bird-food/bird-seeds>

ZooPlus – Parakeets Food

<http://www.zooplus.co.uk/shop/birds/bird_food/large_parakeet>

Index

Q

R

S

T

U

V

W

Photo Credits

Page 1 Photo by Dick Daniels via Wikimedia Commons, <https://commons.wikimedia.org/wiki/File:Rose-ringed_Parakeet_RWD.jpg>

Page 2 Photo by Jim Bendon via Wikimedia Commons, <https://commons.wikimedia.org/wiki/File:Barnardius_zonarius_-Karratha,_Pilbara,_Western_Australia,_Australia-8_(2).jpg>

Page 4 Photo by MinoZig via Wikimedia Commons, <https://commons.wikimedia.org/wiki/File:Psittacula_krameri_Israel.jpg>

Page 9 Photo by J.M.Garg via Wikimedia Commons, <https://commons.wikimedia.org/wiki/File:Rose-ringed_Parakeets_(Male_%26_Female)-_Foreplay_at_Hodal_while_other_males_look_at_I_Picture_0093.jpg>

Page 14 Photo by Manish Kumar via Wikimedia Commons, <https://commons.wikimedia.org/wiki/File:Rose_ringed_parakeet_at_IIT_Delhi.jpg>

Page 16 Photo by south92 via Wikimedia Commons, <https://commons.wikimedia.org/wiki/File:Psittacula_krameri_-colour_mutations_-pets-8a.jpg>

Page 22 Photo by Kamka3000 via Wikimedia Commons, <https://commons.wikimedia.org/wiki/File:Domesticated_Psittacula_krameri.jpg>

Page 26 Photo by Abraham via Wikimedia Commons, <https://commons.wikimedia.org/wiki/File:A_Silesian_Zoological_Garden_105.JPG>

Page 36 Photo by Garry Knight via Wikimedia Commons, <https://commons.wikimedia.org/wiki/File:Psittacula_krameri_-Wimbledon_Common, _London_-female-8.jpg>

Page 44 Photo by J.M.Garg via Wikimedia Commons, <https://commons.wikimedia.org/wiki/File:Rose-ringed_Parakeet_I-Haryana_IMG_9836.jpg>

Page 60 Photo by J.M.Garg via Wikimedia Commons <https://commons.wikimedia.org/wiki/File:Rose-ringed_Parakeets_(Male_%26_Female)-_Foreplay_at_Hodal_I_Picture_0032.jpg>

Page 63 Photo by Chris Biro via Libertywings.com, <http://www.libertywings.com>

Page 66 Photo by Tanya Dropbear via Wikimedia Commons, <https://commons.wikimedia.org/wiki/File:Rose-ringed_Parakeet_(Psittacula_krameri)_-blue_mutation2.jpg>

Page 78 Photo by Shanthanu Bhardwaj via Wikimedia Commons, <https://commons.wikimedia.org/wiki/File:A_Rose-ringed_Parakeet_Psittacula_krameri_in_Gujarat_India_(2).jpg>

Page 84 Photo by William Cho via Wikimedia Commons <https://commons.wikimedia.org/wiki/File:The_Working_Parrot_(300946273).jpg>

References

"About Indian Ringneck/Rose-ringed Parakeet"
ParrotSecrets.com
<http://www.parrotsecrets.com/Indian-Ringneck-Parakeet/about-indian-ringneck-parakeet.php>

"Feeding Your Indian Ringneck or Asiatic Parrot"
IndianRingneck.com
<http://indianringneck.com/feeding/>

"Indian Ring neck" BeautyofBirds.com
<https://www.beautyofbirds.com/indianringneck.html>

"Indian Ringnecks as pets" IndianRingneck.com
<http://indianringneck.com/pet/>

"Indian Ring-Necked Parakeet" Lafeber.com
<https://lafeber.com/pet-birds/species/indian-ring-necked-parakeet/>

"Indian Ringneck Parakeet, Indian Ringneck Parrot, Rose-Ringed Parrot Psittacula krameri" BuffaloBirdNerd.com
<http://www.buffalobirdnerd.com>

"Nestling Development of Ring-necked Parakeets (*Psittacula krameri*) in a Nest Box Population"
by Michael P. Braun and Michael Wink
<http://benthamopen.com>

"Parakeet Origin, History, Information"
Animal-World.com
<http://animalworld.com/encyclo/birds/parakeets/parakeets.htm#Parakeet>

"Rehabilitation of baby Ring-necked parakeets"
RehabbersDen.org
<http://rehabbersden.org>

"Ringneck Parrot Diet" BeautyofBirds.com
<https://www.beautyofbirds.com/ringneckparrotdiet.html>

"Ringneck Parakeet SKU" PETCO Animal Supplies, Inc
<http://mycccbc.org/files/Parakeet_Ringneck_a.pdf>

"Treats for Indian Ring Neck Parrots"
by Jennafer Martin, Demand Media
<http://pets.thenest.com/treats-indian-ring-neck-parrots-10321.html>

"What Is the Difference Between African Ringneck and Indian Ringneck Parrots?"
by Scott Morgan, Demand Media
<http://pets.thenest.com/difference-between-african-ringneck-indian-ringneck-parrots-12187.html>

"Wild birds: Licence to take or kill to prevent damage or disease"
<https://www.gov.uk/government/publications/wild-birds-licence-to-take-or-kill-to-prevent-damage-or-disease>

Feeding Baby
Cynthia Cherry
978-1941070000

Axolotl
Lolly Brown
978-0989658430

Dysautonomia, POTS
Syndrome
Frederick Earlstein
978-0989658485

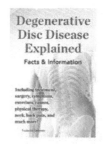

Degenerative Disc
Disease Explained
Frederick Earlstein
978-0989658485

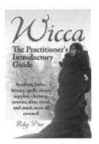

Sinusitis, Hay Fever,
Allergic Rhinitis Explained
Frederick Earlstein
978-1941070024

Wicca
Riley Star
978-1941070130

Zombie Apocalypse
Rex Cutty
978-1941070154

Capybara
Lolly Brown
978-1941070062

Eels As Pets
Lolly Brown
978-1941070167

Scabies and Lice Explained
Frederick Earlstein
978-1941070017

Saltwater Fish As Pets
Lolly Brown
978-0989658461

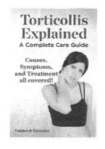

Torticollis Explained
Frederick Earlstein
978-1941070055

Kennel Cough
Lolly Brown
978-0989658409

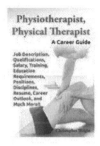

Physiotherapist, Physical
Therapist
Christopher Wright
978-0989658492

Rats, Mice, and Dormice
As Pets
Lolly Brown
978-1941070079

Wallaby and Wallaroo Care
Lolly Brown
978-1941070031

Bodybuilding Supplements
Explained
Jon Shelton
978-1941070239

Demonology
Riley Star
978-19401070314

Pigeon Racing
Lolly Brown
978-1941070307

Dwarf Hamster
Lolly Brown
978-1941070290

Cryptozoology
Rex Cutty
978-1941070406

Eye Strain
Frederick Earlstein
978-1941070369

Inez The Miniature Elephant
Asher Ray
978-1941070353

Vampire Apocalypse
Rex Cutty
978-1941070321